BLINDSIDED
A GAME PLAN FOR GRIEF

BLINDSIDED
A GAME PLAN FOR GRIEF

GLENN AND ROSLYN CRICHTON
& MARK S. M. SCOTT

CLEMENTS PUBLISHING GROUP
TORONTO

BLINDSIDED:
A GAME PLAN FOR GRIEF

Clements Publishing Group Inc.
6021 Yonge Street, Suite 213
Toronto, Ontario M2M 3W2 Canada
www.clementspublishing.com

Cover and interior design by Page Design Inc.
280 Perry St. Unit #8
Peterborough, Ontario K9J 2J4 Canada
www.pagedesign.ca

Library and Archives Canada Cataloguing in Publication

Crichton, Glenn, 1952-
Blindsided: a game plan for grief / Glenn and Roslyn Crichton,
Mark S. M. Scott.

Includes bibliographical references.
ISBN 978–1–926798–29–5

1. Grief therapy. 2. Sports—Psychological aspects. 3. Grief.
4. Sports. I. Scott, Mark S. M. II. Crichton, Roslyn, 1949– III. Title.

RC455.4.L67C75 2013   155.9'37   C2013-901150-1

DEDICATED TO

RACHELE GRACE CRICHTON (1977-1982)

Our beautiful "Chele-Belle," she only lived with us for 5 short years
but changed our lives forever

A. BRIGGS CRICHTON (1919-2011)

My dad inspired me with his passion for life and sports

G & R C

SUSIE LANTZ (1980-2008)

My sister-in-law inspired me with her courage, enthusiasm and
determination

MSMS

"This unique, practical resource fills an important void related to how sports naturally interfaces with times of grief and loss. What an excellent, much needed contribution to a topic that has been ignored for too long. We as humans come to grief when we experience the death of someone loved. The question is: will we be able to openly and honestly mourn. *Blindsided* provides practical illustrations, insights and suggestions to assist the mourner on his or her individual grief journey. Pick this book up now and read it cover to cover; you will be so thankful to learn how to integrate grief into the wide world of sports!"

Alan D. Wolfelt, Ph.D., C.T.
Center for Loss and Life Transition
Fort Collins, Colorado

"This very special and unique book is written for those involved in sports of all stripes, the players, their friends and families, managers, and virtually anyone associated with organized sport. In a creative and practical style, the authors have used familiar athletic experiences in dealing with loss, pain, and competition to inform and sensitively guide how individuals and teams (family) deal with the sudden, often overwhelming impact of death. Born of the pain of their personal losses, and their background and interest in sports, this powerfully written and highly readable volume deals with such crucial topics as: the importance of communication, telling the story of your loss, what to say and what not to say, how to be "present" to someone in their grief, how to honour the deceased's memory and celebrate their life in a meaningful way, how "playing through the pain" in sport informs how you "play through the pain" of loss, and religion and spirituality. In the face of death we frequently don't know where to turn, for those involved in sport and organized teams turn to *Blindsided: A Game Plan for Grief*—it's indispensible."

Stephen Fleming, Ph.D.
Professor of Psychology
Faculty of Health
York University
Toronto, Ontario

"I was working with a professional football team, when the coach's son died. I wish I'd had a clear and concise resource like this book. It contains so many practical steps. More importantly, it articulates the right mindset to adopt for yourself and to encourage in others. I know I'll face the challenge of grief again, both personally and professionally, but now I have a road map for the journey."

Dr. Mike Martin
Registered Psychologist
Former Head of Performance Psychology
Australian Institute of Sport
Paralympic & Olympic Team Psychologist

"It is great to have a book to read which brings grief into the foreground with the athlete in mind. By tackling this taboo in the arena, *Blindsided* helps us continue to skate past the false perception that an athlete is 'soft' if they expose their most vulnerable feelings of hurt and mourning."

Mark Osborne, former NHL player
Detroit, NY Rangers, Toronto & Winnipeg
President - Toronto Maple Leafs Alumni
Leafs TV Host - Pre and Post Game
Hockey Ministries International

"In *Blindsided* the authors draw upon their own experiences of loss and grief to provide a helpful guide through the process in a very practical and meaningful way. It outlines tried and true principles for coping with and expressing grief that will help you begin the life-long process of healing. When I heard the devastating news that my wife of 21 years was suddenly diagnosed with cancer, there was immediate shock and disbelief. In time, the shock and tears faded as we began to turn to practical ways to navigate our 'new normal' and maximize our time together.
May *Blindsided* strengthen and encourage your heart as it did mine."

Laurie Boschman, former NHL Player
Toronto Maple Leafs (first round draft pick),
Edmonton Oilers, Winnipeg Jets, New Jersey
Devils and Ottawa Senators (captain)

TABLE OF CONTENTS

PREFACE

"Courage is not the absence of fear, but the willingness to proceed
in its presence"
—Anonymous

It was midnight when the phone rang. My father-in-law was on the other end of the line: "Mark, we've lost Susie." I sat in stunned silence for a moment. "What happened?" I asked in shock, but I already knew the answer. "There was an accident," he said, plaintively. We dreaded this day would come.

Susie was my sister-in-law, a free spirit who relished athletics and sports, some of them extreme. Years before, when she embarked on an ambitious cycling tour of the western coast of North and South America, we pleaded with her to stay safe, to call often, and to avoid dangerous situations. We made our peace with her departure, knowing that we might not see her again, but, despite several near-misses, she made it back safely with amazing stories of her adventures on the road. We were relieved and we celebrated her impressive accomplishment, even as we still worried about her high-octane, full-tilt, reckless abandon lifestyle. Whatever she did, she did it to the extreme. It was her blessing and curse, and it ultimately led to her demise. It was the phone call my wife and I always dreaded, but somehow thought would never come. Susie was only 28.

We, Glenn and Roslyn, also know what it's like to receive unexpected, life-altering news. When the doctors told us our beautiful little girl was going to die, our lives came to a screeching halt. It was as if the world crumbled around us, and we were left numb, confused, and devastated. As we stood in the hospital room, knowing that Rachele was about to die, those who stood with us in support gave us the courage we needed to face what was ahead, even as our two broken-hearted boys, Adam and Tim, gave us the much needed courage to live as a family one day at a time once we returned home. Over time, we began to discover strategies for coping with grief. In 1990 we founded Coping Bereavement Support Groups of Ontario (COPING), which has been a resource for grieving families for 23 years.

Tragedy often strikes when you least expect it. We (Glenn and Roslyn) were not prepared to face the loss of our daughter. I (Mark) wasn't prepared that night to face the loss of my sister-in-law. We didn't know the toll it would take on our family and friends. Nothing in life can prepare you for those moments. We're thrust into the fog of grief and we're left to grapple in the dark.

Life presents us with turning points or *before and after* moments. They are the events that fundamentally alter our lives. One minute everything's fine, the next our world has fallen apart. One moment we're going in one direction, and then we're forced to dramatically change course. It takes courage to face these moments of loss, and to navigate our way through the changes it brings. If you're an athlete, you know something already about courage under fire. You know what it takes to face difficult challenges. Loss is one of the hardest challenges you'll ever face. But, with time, determination, support, and a game plan, you'll learn to cope with it.

In this short book, we hope to provide you with some practical resources for navigating your grief journey. No two journeys are alike, so we're not attempting to outline *the* roadmap of grief. Instead, we want to sketch some basic principles that might help you find your own path as you cope with your loss. The journey won't be easy, and there are no magic formulas or secret shortcuts, but perhaps we can point you in the right direction as you summon the courage to take your first steps. As they say, a journey of a thousand miles begins . . . with the first step.

ONE

TIMEOUT

When a coach or player signals a "timeout" with the standard "t" hand gesture, you've reached a critical juncture in the game. It's not business as usual. Timeouts give you the time and space to catch your breath, regroup, and mobilize for the difficult task ahead. Sometimes it's helpful to take a timeout in our lives when we're in the midst of a crisis, particularly the death of a friend or family member. When tragedy strikes, it's wise to pause, collect your thoughts and plot the next steps forward. But exactly how should you proceed? It's hard to know what to do and how to feel in the aftermath of loss. Perhaps you question the value of a book about loss. "How depressing!" you might think. In all honesty, you might just want to push it as far as possible out of your mind rather than confront it directly. In the pages ahead we want to help you develop a game plan for grief, drawing principles from the world of sports and our personal experiences with loss.

When a teammate or friend dies, it's difficult to know how to respond, both individually and collectively. What do we do with all the swirling emotions that well up and sometimes overwhelm us? How do we talk about it with our friends and family? What should we do about it? It may have been a frantic couple of days, weeks, or months since the loss of your loved one. Time might have stood still or it might have all been a blur. There's no predictable experience. In these few pages we hope to offer some simple ideas for coping during these difficult days. We can't turn back time or fix what's broken, but we can walk beside you for part of your journey and perhaps point you in a healthy direction for your next steps. Our 30 seconds are up. It's time to get back into the fray.

TWO

BROKEN BONES AND BROKEN HEARTS

"There's a hole in the world now . . . Only a gap remains . . . Only a void is left . . . The world is emptier. My son is gone. Only a hole remains, a void, a gap, never to be filled"

—Nicholas Wolterstorff, *Lament for a Son*, 33

The worst hits are the ones you don't see coming. If you've played sports long enough, especially contact sports, you probably know the jarring pain of unexpected hits. It takes only a moment of distraction or diversion and then . . . BOOM . . . you collide, and it leaves you winded, woozy, and sometimes wounded. When you lose a loved one, whatever the circumstances, it can turn your world upside down. In your collision with loss you might experience emotionally what you've experienced physically after a hard collision: pain, anxiety, anger, disorientation, uncertainty, and fear. If you're reading this book, you probably have lost someone you love or want to assist someone facing loss. We want to encourage you and give you hope. As you read this book we hope that some of the suggestions will help you discover how to mourn in your own unique way.

I'll (Glenn) never forget my first concussion. I was playing Junior Hockey for the Toronto Young Nationals in the Metro Toronto Junior B League. I went into the corner to retrieve the puck and I was blindsided. The next thing I remembered was starring up at the trainer of our team and a couple of my teammates. I had only been knocked out for a short period of time, but I remember the strong feelings of confusion and disorientation. I was dazed and weak-kneed. When I got back to the bench the trainer held up his hand and asked me how many fingers I could see and made me count them. He then broke open a packet of smelling salts, put them under my nose, and asked me if I was okay. When I said "yes" I stayed in the game and continued to play as if nothing had happened.

Over the past few years the sports world has realized the danger and severity of concussions. Before, they were often ignored or not taken too seriously. You certainly wouldn't rest for any length of time to tend to it if you could help it. Now, trainers and doctors are more cautious because of the realization of its impact on the brain. We now know that concussions require lengthy and careful convalescence: a time to heal. If you don't treat it properly and take the necessary time, you risk long-term injury and health issues.

In many ways, sports often imitate life. You might think of grief as a concussion of the heart. It has many of the same symptoms: disorientation, confusion, impairment, and shock. It wasn't that long ago that society's message about loss and grief was to buck up, keep going, and tough it out, but now we know that if we're going to learn to live our lives without the physical presence of the person we have lost, we must take the time to mourn. Dr. Alan Wolfelt, a leading figure in the area of grief and bereavement, describes grief as the inward response to loss and mourning as the outward expression of those feelings. Mourning is the process that enables us to rejoin life in a healthy way.

If we continue to internalize our grief rather than finding ways to express it, we'll suffer more in the long run, like untreated concussions. You shouldn't ignore an injury of the brain and the same goes with the heart. Alan Wolfelt aptly says: "We need to mourn well so we can live well and love well again." The flip side of our grief is love. When we take the time to mourn we honor the lives of the people who have been significant in our lives and make a conscious decision to move towards our grief and to begin to heal.

In the world of grief, healing does not mean the absence of pain or sorrow. Moreover, healing does not mean that we're the same as we were before. It's not a return to the "old normal"; it's an embrace of the "new normal" that emerges in the aftermath of loss. We're forever changed by the people that we love and lose, so healing in the grief process refers to the diverse ways we integrate their loss into our lives.

What is loss? What is grief? How do we cope with loss? These are some of the pressing questions we'll discuss in the following chapters. We'll approach these sensitive issues as fellow travelers on the road to healing, not as experts on the outside with all the answers, especially not with any easy answers. There are no quick fixes for broken hearts, and we make our suggestions not as a way of mapping your grief experience for you, or implying that there's a set pattern of grief or a right or wrong way to mourn (to anticipate: there's not), but only to provide you with resources, both conceptual and practical, that might help you through this difficult time. We've pooled our unique life experiences and our shared love of sports to discuss loss, particularly for athletes and sports enthusiasts.

Before we enter into a conversation with you about loss, allow us to introduce ourselves and to tell you why we're so passionate about the subject. We're three friends who have devoted a lot of time and energy to the reality of loss, both practically and theoretically. In fact, it was loss that brought us together, so we're bound together in friendship by our losses and also by the meaning we've found as we process them. We'll share our stories in the coming chapters, but we should note now that all three of us have experienced the death of family members and we have tried to honor their lives by walking beside others who have lost and helping them to cope with loss in creative, meaningful ways.

Glenn and Roslyn Crichton are the co-founders and directors of Coping (Caring for Other People in Grief) Bereavement and Support Groups of Ontario, which provides group support and a variety of programs for those who have encountered loss. Glenn has an extensive background in sports as a player, coach, manager, and Director of Development for the Ontario Hockey Association. He was appointed as Director of Operations for Team Canada Selects for the prestigious 3 Nations Cup and was awarded the O.H.A gold stick recognizing his contributions to hockey in Ontario. Coping is the bereavement resource for the Ontario Hockey Federation and is called upon to provide support for member partners when a loss occurs within a team. Their Centre has touched thousands of lives. As we'll talk about in the next chapter, their work with bereavement stems from their own profound experience of loss. They bring to our conversation their experiences as educators, facilitators, speakers, and years of experience in the athletic world.

Mark Scott is an author and educator. He's taught, written and spoken about the philosophical and theological problem of evil and suffering in various educational contexts. He received his

Ph.D. from Harvard University and his Masters from Yale Divinity School. He's also an avid sports fan, particularly hockey and baseball. Like Glenn and Roslyn, his work has been motivated by personal loss. The three of us, then, bring together our complementary backgrounds, which will enrich the conversation about what it means to live with loss physically, emotionally, and spiritually.

In *Lament for a Son*, Yale University philosophy professor Nicholas Wolterstorff writes about the loss of his 25-year-old son Eric, who died in a mountain-climbing accident. Wolterstorff's reflections, which are "intensely personal," express the cry of a broken heart. He adopts the theological and literary mode of lament in which he, like Job and the writer of the Psalms before him, gives voice to his anger, fear, frustration, and despair. You also begin to see the first light of hope that dawns in his heart as he gradually adjusts to his new reality and begins to see it in new ways over time. As he shares his powerful and intimately personal story and thoughts on the loss of his son, the reader instantly and instinctively makes connections with his or her own grief experience.

From his short, poignant book we see the value of giving expression to grief, of sharing your grief story, and of finding ways to do "the work of mourning," as we'll discuss more in the subsequent pages. Everybody's story of loss is different. Everybody's experience of grief is different. And yet, amid these differences, there's something common, something shared in the experience of loss, something that unites us. Wolterstorff touches on this mystery of unity amid plurality in loss: "What I have learned, to my surprise, is that in its particularly there is universality" (*Lament for a Son*, 5). If this is true, then we have a deep connection with you, the reader, and if that's the case, then as we tell our stories and offer our insights, we hope that you'll be empowered and inspired to tell your story and that you'll be encouraged to begin the long journey of coping with your loss, together with us and with those around you. Your grief belongs to you alone, but you're not alone in your grief. Let's talk about that next.

THREE

LOSS AND GRIEF

"Her absence was like the sky, spread over everything"

— C. S. Lewis, *A Grief Observed*

In sports, losses sometimes really hurt. You train hard to win, so to fall short of the prize stings. When you've invested a lot of time, money, and effort, losses leave their mark. There's a great line from the movie *Moneyball* where Billy Beane (played by Brad Pitt) says: "I hate losing more than I like winning." You know what that feels like if you've experienced tough losses in competition. It's an empty, angry, bitter, sinking feeling. You'd do almost anything to go back in time to have another chance to seize the victory.

Now I (Mark) must make a full confession to you. In all honesty, I'm not a gracious loser. In the past at least, I have not *always* suffered loss with calm, composure, and sportsmanship. I have been known to throw my ping-pong racket, toss the game board, break my hockey stick or baseball bat, declare the victory illegitimate for various questionable technicalities, and storm off the field, as it were. At least, that's how I was in my hyper-competitive younger days, and I'd like to think I face those rare occasions of loss in sports and competition with more maturity now, but you would have to ask my friends and family about that. At any rate, I know exactly what Billy Beane means.

Loss is not easy even in the recreational world of sports. But here we're talking about real life loss, and that's far more difficult. You may have endured tough losses in your sports career, but now you're facing a loss of far greater magnitude. And this loss, well, this loss makes the loss of a Game 7 in overtime pale into insignificance. It's probably the toughest loss you've ever encountered, and it might leave you reeling. What is loss? How does it impact us? How do we deal with it? Stories, as you will see, are powerful mediums to convey and process loss, so let's begin with our story of loss.

Life was turning out as I (Roslyn) had always dreamed it would as a young girl living in Sydney, Australia. I had married Glenn, a Canadian—the man of my dreams—and had settled in Canada after spending the first three years of our marriage in Australia. Our lives became even happier and more complete with the arrival over the next few years of our three children: Adam, Rachele and Tim. Glenn was busy climbing the corporate ladder and playing Senior A hockey. Life was perfect. It was the Civic Holiday weekend in 1982 when we noticed Rachele, almost five years old, had some swollen glands in her neck. A visit to the doctor on Tuesday prompted him to do a blood test. On Wednesday she seemed perfectly fine and was doing cartwheels in the family room. That evening as I tucked her into bed she seemed to be breathing heavily and I wondered if she was developing a respiratory infection. When she awoke in the morning she complained of a sore stomach. I called the doctor and asked if there were any results from the blood test. He said he had just received them and her white blood cell count was high and he would make an afternoon appointment with the pediatrician to check it out. He suggested I bring her pajamas in case she had to stay overnight. At this point I was not thinking it was anything too serious. Rachele had always been a healthy little girl.

I phoned Glenn to let him know what was happening and told him I would call him after I saw the pediatrician. Rachele looked well and was quite energetic. The pediatrician examined Rachele and walked out of the room and said he would be right back. Through the window in the door I saw the doctor put his head in his hands and in that moment I knew something was very wrong and my heart began to race. He returned, squared his shoulders and looked directly at me. The words he was about to speak would be words I would hear in my head a hundred times. He told me Rachele had lymphoblastic leukemia. The room spun around me and I began to cry. Rachele grabbed my hand and asked why I was crying. I had a deep sense that our lives would never be the same from that moment on. My sense was right. The nightmare began on August 5, 1982. We needed to take Rachele to the Children's Hospital in London immediately. I made the most difficult phone call of my life to Glenn to tell him the terrible news.

I (Glenn) remember being a little concerned about Rachele after the initial phone call from Roslyn about Rachele's appointment with the pediatrician but nothing could prepare me for the second call. Roslyn was on the other end crying. She could hardly get the words out. It only took a few seconds for the news to sink in. I felt my knees buckle under me and I could feel the strength being zapped from my body. I became somewhat robotic as I went into my boss's office to tell him I had to leave immediately. I am not sure how I found my way to the hospital, but I remember the sense of fear, panic, and despair that overtook me. I remember sobbing uncontrollably and then audibly crying out, "What have we ever done to deserve this?!" Someone had to be at fault and somehow in my state of shock and confusion I felt that I must have been responsible.

The nightmare only grew worse at the hospital. They administered chemotherapy on August 7th and Rachele's condition began to deteriorate. A terrible feeling of helplessness gripped me. Surely as a dad I could—I must!—find a solution, a way to fix this problem. That's a basic instinct of all parents: to mend wounds, to cure illness, and to alleviate the pain of our children, but this disease knew no boundaries. I remember sitting by her bedside begging God to let me take her place. I would have traded places with her in a heartbeat if that meant she would be spared. Sleep eluded me. I was haunted by the debilitating fear of what the day would hold for us. The situation was spinning out of control and no matter what I tried to do things just were getting worse and worse.

By Sunday it was evident that Rachele was not going to live and we could see the impact of the disease on her body. Watching her suffer was devastating and it was then that I cried out that I would rather suffer the rest of my life than see her suffer for one more moment. Rachele died on Monday, August 9th. Our family members who stood with us in solidarity during that terrible five-day trauma share a bond with us that will last forever.

Driving home from the hospital without her with us was excruciating beyond words. As I (Roslyn) looked out the window and saw cars driving up and down the highway, people going in and out of coffee shops, I wanted to scream. I wanted the world to stop! Our daughter had just died and yet the world was continuing on as if nothing had happened. I felt like I had come to a screaming halt. In the weeks and months that followed the funeral there were so many overwhelming emotions flooding in and yet we had to somehow keep going. I wanted the world to stop for just a while so we could get off and catch our breath.

I often felt robotic, doing the daily tasks that make up most of our days but not really experiencing them. It was like being disconnected from myself, being outside of my body as I was going through the motions of life. I felt like an alien surrounded by earthlings. The yearning for Rachele was unbearable. The pain was indescribable. It seemed like I was totally preoccupied with what happened to Rachele and it took an enormous amount of energy to focus on everyday living. Exhaustion, lack of concentration, and feeling like I was riding a rollercoaster became my normal. I found it difficult to recall the happy memories with Rachele. They were bittersweet. It seemed like all I could think of were those five days in the hospital. While I needed to talk about what had happened and about Rachele, I hid a lot of my feelings because I wasn't sure what I should do with them.

My faith in knowing Rachele was in heaven brought me a great deal of peace, but it did not take away the pain of missing her every moment of every day. The yearning to have her on my lap, give her a hug, and talk to her was powerful. As a public speaker I slowly began to talk about the experience of loss and what it was teaching me about myself and others. In this process I began to sort out a lot of my thoughts and feelings and realize now that I was beginning to mourn Rachele, often in a public setting. Over the next eight years I began to speak to hundreds of the bereaved and learned about their unique experiences of loss. It became more and more obvious to us that in most cases the needs of grieving families were not being adequately met.

I (Glenn) returned from the hospital and immersed myself in all the tasks of preparing for the funeral. I found it helpful to be busy and it gave me something tangible to do, which I think I needed at that point. In many ways I was not prepared to give up being Rachele's dad even after she had died, and it was important for me to help plan the funeral. It gave me a small measure of control amid the chaos of those days, and as her father it was something I could do to stay as close to her as I possibly could. The thought of saying goodbye to a little girl that we had only had for five short years was excruciating. How could I say goodbye when I hadn't even had a long enough time to say hello? I remember saying to Roslyn that if we can just get some time between her death, funeral and the rest of our lives things might be just as they were before and everything would be all right. I hadn't come to realize yet that we would be changed forever.

I remember thinking that my role as a father and husband was to fix everything for my family and I invested all my energies to that end. I got very busy that year taking the head coaching job of the Cambridge Hornets, building a new home, and accepting a promotion at work. I think I bought into the myth of "out of sight, out of mind." I found all my energy going into trying to repress all my emotions rather than finding ways to express them. I became emotionally and physically exhausted. I was coaching but had just retired from playing and still would enjoy going out for a game of scrimmage. It was during one of those games that I found myself taking opposing players into the boards much harder than necessary in a scrimmage for fun; somehow I was hoping that one of the opposing players would drop the gloves and a fight might ensue. I didn't care if I won or lost the fight, I just needed an outlet for all my pent-up emotions. In hindsight I realize that by actively repressing my grief, it only re-emerged in unhealthy ways.

It began to slowly dawn on me that my grief was bigger than me and that if I didn't consciously determine to slow down and turn toward my grief instead of repressing it, that my emotions would continue to manifest themselves in unhealthy and unproductive ways. I began to notice that gradually I was developing a whole new value system. Things that had been important to me before were not that important to me now. There was nothing wrong with my old value system; it just didn't fit into my new world. It occurred to me that my family didn't need fixing. You can't fix broken hearts and it wasn't my job to fix everyone. It became clearer to me that even though we had all lost the same person, each of us would mourn her differently and if I wanted to support my family I needed to give them permission to honor their unique relationship with Rachele.

When you lose someone close to you, it transforms your life forever. For you, the world has changed. Your relational landscape has been altered dramatically. There is a void in the space they filled. It forces you to renegotiate your reality, to learn how to live without their presence in your life. It's not an easy prospect or process, and it takes time to adjust to your new circumstance without them. We need to learn to trust this process and to be patient and compassionate with ourselves. Often the world around us puts pressure on grieving people to get over their grief in certain time frames. Healing does not come quickly and our work of mourning is never fully completed, but our grief does change. Time does not heal all wounds, but what we do with the time allows us to live life with meaning and purpose, always remembering and honoring the person that we have lost.

We hope these stories impress upon you that you're not alone. Grief is intensely personal, but it does not have to isolate you.

People often say: "It's okay, I know how you feel," but it's not okay and nobody knows exactly how you feel. Every loss is irreducibly unique. It reflects your special history with that person and your emotional response to their absence. It cannot be duplicated, and no one has access to another's inner life. And yet, others have lost loved ones and their experience allows the possibility of communion with you in your loss, not because they "know how you feel" exactly, but because they know what it is to have lost someone. And, if we're willing to tell our story and others are willing to listen respectfully and attentively, we're able to clear some common ground. Ironically, despite its distinctiveness at the individual level, it remains a common—even fundamental—human experience. So, upon deeper reflection, the very thing that might seem to isolate us actually brings us together once we realize that loss is something we all must face at some point. You might feel very alone right now, but remember there are people out there to help you: friends, family, caregivers, and others. You need to reach out to them and accept their help if they're reaching out to you.

Coping with loss is a marathon, not a sprint. There are no prizes for finishing first because there's no finish line and there are no competitors. In the 100-meter sprint in the Olympics we witness athletes running at top speed toward the finish line to win the gold. Their speed amazes us and we admire their competitive spirit. In grief, however, we're not racing against anyone, and there's no destination other than the ongoing integration of our loss into our new reality. It takes time to adjust to the new normal of life without our loved one. Grief is not always progressive, sometimes it involves forward and backward motion, so you need to pace yourself emotionally and perhaps adjust your expectations.

It's important to take care of yourself physically, emotionally, and spiritually during your grief. Take time to do some of the "normal" activities you did before your loss. Sleep or eat if you're able. Maybe take an afternoon off and try to do something that you find enjoyable and peaceful. Don't try to process all your feelings at once. Give yourself permission to take breaks. You need breaks along the way, stations to rest and revive yourself so that you can continue on your journey. Don't try to accelerate the emotional healing because you can't fast-track grieving, just as you can't fast-track the healing and rehabilitation of a physical injury. It's not a sprint; it's more of a marathon. Like every seasoned marathon runner, you'll eventually find your stride and discover your second wind, but let it happen gradually and organically, don't rush the process. Let's take some time now to explore how you can receive support from others in your grief journey.

FOUR

TEAM AS COMMUNITY

"We are one in suffering. Some are wealthy, some bright; some athletic, some admired. But we all suffer"

— Nicholas Wolterstorff, *Lament for a Son,* 89

You win as a team and you lose as a team. Every good coach will tell you that. It's the central principle of team sports: you have to work together to accomplish your goals. Sometimes you win, sometimes you lose, but you do it as a unit. Everybody has a role, a part to play, and success often depends on how well each person executes the game plan. Being part of a team gives you a sense of identity and belonging. It's a powerful feeling. The relationships forged in team sports stay with you well after the games have ended.

How does the concept of team help us in grief? Well, first, if the person you lost was part of your team, you share their loss with your teammates. You all miss the person in your own way, but it impacts the entire team. You mourn together. Loss is an emotional burden and your team can help you carry that by their presence, by sharing in conversation with you about your lost loved one, and by helping with practical needs. Likewise, you can help your teammates with their struggles if they're open to it. A team is a community. There's a camaraderie and intimacy that transcends sports.

Of course, not all athletes play team sports, but even in individual sports there's a sense of community among the competitors. You may not have competed together as a team, but your shared love of and involvement with a sport gives you a sports community that you can draw on in your loss, and that you can contribute to when others lose a loved one. We need to support each other as best as we can. Listen to each other. Spend time with each other. Ask for and give any practical help that's needed. You're a team, and a good team finds a way to meet challenges and pull together when the going gets tough. It utilizes the diverse strengths of its individual members to create something that's bigger than the sum of its parts: a supportive community.

You've heard the popular saying "there's no 'I' in 'team,'" which means that the individual must sacrifice his or her personal glory for the good of the team. It's not about individual statistics or accolades, it's about the victory for the team. Individuals are in the background, team objectives are in the foreground. That's standard procedure in sports. In grief, however, it's inverted. When it comes to coping with loss, there IS an "I" in "team" because the good of the team consists in the good of every person's journey through grief. Rather than sacrifice the individual for the sake of the team, we attend to individual needs, struggles, and expressions of grief for the sake of the team. It's not that the team no longer matters after loss; it's that the team flourishes and succeeds when it provides a context for each person's unique grief experience to express itself.

Something special happens to a team when they have spent a great deal of time together. Gradually, the players begin to think of each other as family. Standing shoulder to shoulder in the heat of battle forges deep bonds in competitive sports. These are deepened further when they face loss in real life. They move from a community to something more profound: a family. Your sports family includes coaches, staff, girlfriends/boyfriends, and all the other people associated with the team. When the team becomes a family, it faces the same problems that occur when loss hits your biological family: people cope differently and it puts stress on the relationships. As a family, you must allow every person to grieve in their own way, not expect everyone to process it in exactly the same way. Also, you must pull together as a family to get through the difficult days ahead, hand-in-hand. Family always takes care of family, particularly in tough times, and a team is a family.

Communities provide safety, stability, and support for us in our grief journeys. Grieving is intrinsically and intensely personal, but you need not walk alone. As you process your grief, look for ways to include others. Your teammates and other sports colleagues are important emotional and relational resources. They're there to help you, if you trust them and yourself enough to lean on them. But where do you begin? In sports, communication is essential to success. Similarly, in grief, communication helps us tell our story of loss and begin to process it. Let's turn next to the power of story in the grief journey.

FIVE

COMMUNICATION AND THE POWER OF STORY

"I will not say do not weep, for not all tears are an evil"

—J. R. R. Tolkien, *The Lord of the Rings*

"Let's talk out there, boys," you might hear someone say on the bench during a game. Outfielders call for the ball to avoid confusions and collisions. Players yell for the puck or the basketball so that their teammates know they're open. Athletes of every description draw up plays, warn of danger, and improvise through constant communication. In sports as in life, communication is crucial. It's the key ingredient to successful relationships, business, academics, art and so many other areas of life. And yet, when it comes to feelings, many athletes keep a stiff upper lip. There's a pervasive culture of silence: you don't express your feelings because it's a sign of weakness. You worry you might be mocked, and sometimes you just don't know how to put your feelings into words.

We know that success on the playing field requires communication in various forms. Elite athletes master the art of communication in their respective sports. Similarly, in the grief process, communication plays a central role. How might the principle of communication in sports translate into the realm of grief? We want to begin with a few practical suggestions before we talk about it in detail. First, it's important for the team to create an atmosphere of trust and confidence. You won't share your feelings if you feel judged or think someone might share them outside the confines of the locker room without your authorization. Second, the team could create a specific forum for players to voice their thoughts and feelings. It doesn't have to be formal or overly structured. It's important to create a safe space for players to express themselves. Finally, teams should provide support and resources to players for talking about their grief.

Communication in grief often involves sharing our struggles with loss. For athletes this might be difficult. Many have been brought up with a "suck it up buttercup" approach to pain, where you pull up your bootstraps on your own, put on your game face and play through the pain in silence. Playing with pain is part of sports and part of grief—we live with the pain of loss—but silence need not be part of that equation. There's no shame in asking for help. There's no weakness in admitting fear, anger, pain and confusion. There's no defeat in sharing your struggles. Loss is difficult, and sometimes it leaves us flat on our backs. That's when a teammate comes and offers a hand to lift you up. That's the strength of any good team: they pick each other up in difficult times. If you refused the outstretched hand of your teammate as you lay on the ice or field, you wouldn't be stronger because of that, you would be weaker, and so would the team that needs you. Athletes are often wary of emotional vulnerability, but try to see the expression of your feelings of loss and your struggles with loss not as a sign of weakness but as an invitation to allow others to mourn with you and to open yourself up to their comfort and presence.

Another way to translate communication into the realm of grief is to talk about the power of story. We're intuitively drawn to stories. That's why we watch movies, read books, listen to music and see plays about the lives of others, both real and fictional. Stories are the prism through which we see and interpret or own existence. In grief, telling the story of our loss allows us to give a verbal tribute to those we have lost, to affirm their enduring importance in our lives. It also gives us a medium to process their loss in our lives. By talking about them and their importance to us, we begin to adjust to life without them even as they, paradoxically, remain present to us through the telling of story.

Let me (Mark) tell you my story of loss. When I was a teenager my girlfriend's mother died tragically a few days before Christmas in 1996. She was crossing the road on a foggy night around twilight to visit her ailing mother at the hospital when she was hit by a truck. She parked across the road from the hospital to avoid paying the two-dollar parking fee. Two of her daughters were with her, but thankfully neither was hurt. Three years later that girlfriend became my wife, so it was really the loss of my future mother-in-law. Her name was Ruth Ann Lantz (Evans) and she was very special. She was known for her big hugs, ready smile, straight-talk advice, and deep friendships. She was the heartbeat of her church and her family. Her husband and four daughters basked in the glow of her love. Although she was not rich or famous, she left a rich legacy of love and joy to her family, friends, and church. Her tragic death left her family in turmoil: they were never the same. My wife met with Roslyn during this time to help her cope with her profound loss, and that was the beginning of our friendship with them and their family.

About 12 years later, my sister-in-law, Susie Lantz, also died tragically in a backcountry skiing accident. She was skiing down a mountain that was not a ski resort when she was caught in a sudden avalanche. It was another crushing blow for a family still reeling from the loss of their mother. You should never have to watch a father bury his daughter; it's heartbreaking. Susie was an inspiring person. She once embarked on an epic journey from British Columbia to South America on her bike, mostly by herself (against our pleas). She was known for her love of life and adventure, her drive and determination, her energy and encouragement, and her silly sense of humor. When she was visiting us after the birth of our firstborn, my wife would send us out on little errands and we would have fun trying to track down her very specific list of items. When we got it wrong we always took turns blaming each other, and we would go out again to get it right. It's strange the little, seemingly trivial, things you remember with fondness. We all miss her every day.

When I reflect on their lives and untimely deaths, it triggers a lot of conflicting emotions. I feel anger because their deaths were completely preventable: they were the direct result of their own carelessness. I feel sadness over the suffering it caused my wife, father-in-law, sister-in-laws, and our extended network of family and friends. I deeply regret that Ruth and I did not have the opportunity share our lives together as an extended family. Ruth would have been a wonderful grandmother. She would have been so proud of her four daughters and she would have adored her seven (at present) beautiful grandchildren. I feel sad that Susie didn't have the chance to meet two of my children, that I didn't get to meet the children she might have had in later years, and that I was too critical of her full-tilt lifestyle, when really I admired her for it. At the same time, I'm grateful for the time we shared together, for our long conversations on the phone, and for her many visits with us. And I'm grateful for Ruth's mothering and for the impressive women she raised.

As you can see, the emotions that arise from telling my story of loss are all over the map. Telling your story does not have to be systematic, neat, or have a happy ending. Feelings don't follow a script. Telling your story gives you an opening into your grief. It's a release valve for your emotions and a window into greater insights on the significance of that person to your life. In small, perhaps imperceptible ways, it helps you adjust to the "new normal" of life without them. Your story of grief will be different from ours, but as you hear them perhaps you will find points of contact that will help you discover and tell your story, and that might be a good first step toward healing.

SIX

PRESENCE AS SOLIDARITY

"To comfort me, you have to come close. Come sit beside me on my mourning bench"

— Nicholas Wolterstorff, *Lament for a Son*, 34

Something strange happens to players when they've reached the pinnacle of professional accomplishment. In the aftermath of their biggest victory, they're struck by stunned silence. Whether it's sipping from the Stanley Cup, hoisting the Vince Lombardi or Commissioner's trophy, or starring intently at their gold medal, it opens up a floodgate of emotions that overwhelms them. It's the culmination of a lifetime of hard work, sacrifice, and determination, and when they finally reach the summit, they can't describe the view. With the cameras rolling, the Champagne flowing, and the players embracing, they suddenly become totally dumbstruck. "Describe this moment. How do you feel?" an interviewer will ask. "I don't know. I'm speechless. I can't put it into words right now," they respond, with a dazed look in their eyes. It's always heartwarming to watch.

Athletes are not always known for their soaring rhetoric. In fact, it's usually the opposite: they simply repeat the standard repertoire of sports platitudes: "We have to go out there and give 110%. We need to take it one game at a time. We have to keep it simple. We have to work together. We need to go out there and have some fun again." You've heard them all before. Their speechlessness at these moments of triumph reveals that in the face of overwhelming emotion, we often don't know what to say; we're at a loss for words. The same applies to deep emotion at the other end of the spectrum. In moments of loss, words fail us. They don't seem up to the task. They ring hollow, fall short, and come up empty. We know the feeling internally, we just don't have the words to express it.

In the last section we spoke about the importance of communication, of creating a space for players to talk about loss as a team and in other group and private contexts. Expression takes on many different forms: verbal, writing, projects, art, and music, for instance. Finding ways to express your feelings of grief and sharing your story of loss are critical steps in the healing process. At some point, however, words aren't up to the job. You just don't know what to say, and neither do your family and friends. You hit a wall where there just isn't anything more to say. When words fail, the presence of teammates, family members, and friends serve an invaluable function.

Most people don't know what to say to a person in grief. In fact, you may have noticed that some people seem awkward and uncomfortable around you, especially if you've experienced a loss recently. It's almost as if you're emotionally radioactive: many keep a safe distance to avoid contamination. In all likelihood, that's because they want to comfort you, but they have absolutely no idea where to begin, and that might scare them. Here we want to talk about what NOT to say to a person in grief, about the role of silence, and about the power of presence to show solidarity with those in the grip of grief.

People say all sorts of hurtful things in the aftermath of loss. Some of it comes from a sincere but misguided desire to help by diminishing the pain, and some of it comes from the fact that we're unpracticed in talking about death. We don't have enough experience to know what to say and what not to say. We're sympathetic to that because we know that people often scramble for words of comfort and, in the pressure of the moment, blurt out comments that are unhelpful at best and hurtful at worst. In our society we don't talk about death much—we're still very much a death-denying and death-ignoring society—so when we're thrust into a situation where we're face-to-face with death, we're simply out of our depth because of our lack of experience. It's all right if you don't know what to say to a bereaved person, but try to avoid clichés or glib comments. Measure your words. We've heard so many unhelpful comments that it's hard to narrow it down to a "don't say" list, but here are a few things grieving people have shared with us through the years.

Don't say "it could be worse" because that minimizes the loss. Don't say "I know how you feel" because you don't know exactly how they feel, even if you've experienced loss. Every person's inner life belongs to them alone, and only when they share their feelings with you can you *begin* to appreciate how they feel. Don't say "it is God's will" because you do not know the mind of God or the beliefs of the person you're attempting to console. Don't say "get over it" because grief is not something you "get over" but something you learn to live with. It does not have an expiration date.

Here are a few more unhelpful comments that we've encountered that should be avoided. "Now you're the man of the house, look after your mom." That kind of commission places an undo burden on a hurting child that only compounds the pain. "Time will heal." Time enables us to work through our grief, but time alone does not heal the loss. "Thank goodness you have another child." To a bereaved parent this comment minimizes the enormity of their loss, as if the child were replaceable. "At least he/she is not suffering anymore." Again, these types of statements tend to minimize the loss in an effort to ease the pain. In the aftermath of loss, however, we have to acknowledge the pain, to confront it head on, not dismiss or attenuate it by some faulty "it's not so bad" perspective.

There are some things you might say, and we'll share just a few of them as pointers in case you've wondered what you should say. Affirm your love for them. Tell them you're thinking about and praying for them. Acknowledge the depth of the loss, don't minimize it. Share a meaningful memory of the person who died. Talk about how they impacted your life in a positive way or inspired you in some way. Ask them if there's anything you can do for them. Above all, say little unless you're invited to say more and speak from the heart. Be a listening ear. Your presence is more important than your words. Eventually words come up empty, and that's when the power of presence fills in the gap. Let us give you a personal example of how presence soothes when words fail.

Dean Prentice spent 22 years in the NHL. He was a member of one of the most successful lines in the history of the New York Rangers (Bathgate, Prentice, Popein). In 1966 he was traded to the Detroit Red Wings and became part of another famous line in the history of the Detroit Red Wings (Howe, Delvechio, Prentice). Dean was known for his hard work, consistent play every shift, and his quiet and unassuming personality. He subsequently has been recognized as one of the most underrated players of his era.

After his retirement, Dean and June moved to Cambridge where we (Glenn and Roslyn) got to know them on a personal basis. When Rachele died I (Glenn) don't remember anything anyone said to me that took away my pain and suffering or made me feel better, but there was one person who sticks out in my mind that provided comfort, but not through words. That person was Dean Prentice. Each day Dean would come to the house and sit in the corner of the room. I am sure that we spoke but I don't remember what we talked about. What I do remember is that I didn't feel quite as alone when Dean came into the room. Later I came to realize that Dean had given one of the best gifts of comfort that we can give each other. It's the gift of presence. Dean didn't try to fix me, he didn't try to take my pain away and he wasn't trying to provide me with any clichés or advice. He simply showed up. Dean's simple presence brought comfort to my broken heart.

If you are struggling with what to do or say, or feel pressure or uncomfortable in going to a funeral or visitation, that's okay. Remember the lessons that Dean Prentice taught us. Dean brought comfort by being present, and you also can bring comfort and receive comfort by being present with others or having others be present for you.

What does it mean to be present to someone in their grief? We'll give you two practical suggestions. First, it might involve attending to their practical needs. Death brings all sorts of practical problems in addition to emotional stress. From funeral arrangements to meals to housing those from out-of-town, a host of unexpected details and difficulties arise. Ask how you can be helpful. Many people ask as a formality without really intending to help, but when you ask, say you really mean it and perhaps suggest a few concrete ways to help. We've seen people express their love, support and solidarity by paying for funeral or other related expenses, organizing or participating in the funeral, bringing over meals, and all sorts of other things. These are excellent ways to "sit on the mourning bench" with someone in their grief. They're often too overwhelmed with emotion to handle these details, so it's extremely helpful when someone steps in to help.

Second, presence means actually being there for them to listen to them and to support them in whatever way you can. In sports, we're taught the value of "showing up." You "show up" for practice, "show up" for the big game, and "show up" for your team in various ways, such as fundraising. In the face of loss, we need to show up for our friends and family too, not fade into the background. I (Mark) remember when my wife's mother died, some of her friends drove from many hours away in dangerously inclement weather to attend the funeral. She doesn't remember a word they said, but she remembers that they showed up. Some things in life matter more than others. You show up for funerals and you show up to help friends through the difficult days afterwards by your presence. Let us share a story of loss and coming together that exemplifies the power of presence.

Ben Pearson was a gifted athlete who channeled his energies into hockey. He was a talented player, a leader on and off the ice, and a fan favorite. He was (and is) deeply loved by his family, friends, and teammates. Ben embarked on a rigorous physical training program to increase his strength, speed, and stamina for the upcoming hockey season. Part of that routine included a high protein diet to build muscle and strength. Ben was not aware that his body did not contain an enzyme necessary to break down protein in his digestive system. Ben felt ill during one of his games and very quickly deteriorated over a five-day period. The loss of Ben blindsided everyone that knew him. It was a profound loss, but amid their pain his family, friends, and teammates pulled together to honor his memory, celebrate his life, and help each other get through some tough days.

Ben's funeral was held in the local arena with his coffin at centre ice. The local church that Ben's mom had attended was invaluable in assisting with the funeral arrangements and conducting the funeral. Ben's closest friends spoke at his memorial service. All the teams that Ben had played for wore their team sweaters. The players on Ben's team built a Stanley Cup out of the tins of Ben's favorite chewing tobacco and placed it in his stall in the dressing room. Ben's sweater was retired by his team in a special ceremony and hung from the rafters of the building. The rink Zamboni was repainted with Ben's name on it to preserve his memory during the hockey games. His teammates created a scrapbook of all the newspaper clippings of Ben's hockey exploits and gave it to his family, and the team presented the family with Ben's last team picture. These and other thoughtful acts done in honor and memory of Ben demonstrate the power of presence to bring people together to cope with loss. They "showed up" for each other, and for him.

Despite whatever anxiety or sense of inadequacy you might have, resolve to be there for your bereaved friends and family as an expression of love and solidarity with them in their grief. You don't have to be perfect. Don't put too much pressure on yourself. Just try to be thoughtful and helpful, that's all. Let them take the lead in conversation, allowing them to teach you what the loss means to them. Don't monopolize their time. Instead, be mindful about when to come and go and how long you stay, but keep the lines of communication open and show that you're ready to sit beside them on the mourning bench. Your actions speak louder than your words. Speak only when necessary, and never as a way to diminish or explain away their loss. Your presence does not take away their pain, but it does allow you to share in their pain, at least in part, and that's often an enormous comfort to those reeling from loss. Without words, it says to them: "This sucks and I can't make it better, but I care about you and I'm here for you." As they say, people don't care how much you know until they know how much you care.

SEVEN

LEGACY AND CELEBRATION

"If ever there comes a day when we can't be together keep me in your heart. I will stay there forever"

— Winnie the Pooh

Bobby Orr and Wayne Gretzky. Frankie Robinson and Babe Ruth. Jerry Rice and Joe Montana. Magic Johnson and Michael Jordan. Muhammad Ali, LeBron James, Tiger Woods, Roger Federer, the Williams sisters, Pele and the list goes on and on and on. What do these elite athletes all have in common, aside from the fact that they were iconic players in their respective sports? The answer is: they all left a lasting legacy that shaped their sport and defined an era. When great athletes retire or pass away, commentators on ESPN or TSN talk about their contribution to the sport, their significance to the game and their defining moments. Often they'll retire the player's number in a lavish ceremony full of pomp and pageantry, or they'll name a trophy, award, or sometimes even a building after them. We celebrate the accomplishments of our sports heroes, and great players are conscious of the fact that their play on and off the ice, field, court, etc., slowly crafts a legacy that will define them for the rest of their life and well beyond.

The truth is, however, that we all leave behind a legacy, even if we're not sports celebrities. You don't have to be rich or famous to have a legacy. Everybody impacts the world around them, and our legacy will be the culmination of our aspirations, decisions, and associations. Most of our lives will go unheralded. We probably won't make any top ten lists of the greatest all-time players. And yet, the way we live our lives has a ripple effect on the world around us, and with every decision we make, every life we touch, and every goal we achieve, we imprint our legacy on the world around us. So we're wise to ask ourselves about the status of our legacy: "What kind of legacy am I building by the way I live, the way I carry myself, and by the kind of person I am becoming?"

So legacies reflect the unique characteristics and contributions of the person, in sports as in life. When a teammate or fellow athlete dies, then, we should ask ourselves: "What is their legacy, both in sports and in life, and how do I honor it?" Every person impacts the world differently with their distinctive personality and gifts. What were some of the best qualities or traits of the person you lost? What were some of their defining moments in sports and some of their defining characteristics? By asking these questions, you're drilling down to the bedrock of their personality and into the core of their impact on your life. What made them so special to you, and how can you express that and remember that? As we've spoken about earlier, one way to honor them is to talk about them and their legacy in your life. Another way to honor their memory and preserve their legacy, however, is through concrete acts of remembrance that fit with our own personalities. There are all sorts of ways to do this. It requires creativity and collaboration, which helps us focus our thoughts on the person we lost and come together to honor their memory.

For instance, if he or she were an avid tennis player, you could raise funds and build a community tennis court in his or her memory, which might reflect both their interest in tennis and their contribution to the community. If they loved baseball you could start a fund for underprivileged children to go to baseball camp. If they were part of the football team you could wear their jersey number or dedicate a game to them. The possibilities are endless. Honoring their legacy requires reflection on their life (which might be painful) and creativity in thinking about how to do something that expresses their uniqueness. You honor their memory and preserve and perpetuate their legacy by these concrete acts, which become part of the mourning process for you and for others. What we're talking about is called the "work of mourning," where you not only discuss your grief and tell your story, but also "do" tangible things to remember them. There's no set formula for the work of mourning, but let us give you two examples of preserving and honoring a person's legacy, one individual, the other collective.

Once we (Roslyn and Glenn) visited a school where an 11-year-old athlete died very unexpectedly and suddenly. He attended the school because of his athletic ability and he was very popular among the students and staff alike. We spoke to the student body about his loss and we also spoke to individual classes. During one of these more intimate class discussions about coping with the loss of their classmate and teammate, a friend of his relayed to us the importance of their friendship and shared with the class his resolve to make his life count as a tribute to him, since his friend would not have the same opportunity. His resolution illustrates the power of legacy. A person leaves us a legacy when their lives have changed us and our value systems. His determination to make his life count in memory of and in tribute to his friend also teaches us about the ways we continue to honor those we have loved and lost by grafting them into our lives through these sorts of acts of significance.

Another example of honoring and celebrating legacy comes to us from the friends and family of Ben Pearson. To honor Ben's memory his friends and family organized an annual golf tournament to raise funds for a player scholarship as well as for the Coping Centre to sponsor grieving children to attend the Adventure Camp. Many people in the community donated prizes and sponsorships for the tournament, rallying around the family and joining together to remember his life and his legacy. As well, a number of Ben's teammates had a special tattoo designed in memory of Ben. They also made a commemorative bench out of hockey sticks to put in the memory garden at the Coping Center. In the second year of the tournament 180 of Ben's friends came together to support the family and remember Ben. Friends designed a special logo for hats and t-shirts that incorporated Ben's passions, and everyone wore them. A memory area was set up at the Coping Centre with Ben's friends coming and providing the labor. So we see in the partnership between his friends and family the variety of concrete ways they preserve his memory, honor his life, and positively impact the community.

We encourage you to find ways to continue the legacy of your fallen teammate, friend or loved one. It does not have to be extravagant or expensive. Personalize your activity to express your relationship with them and their unique spirit. Brainstorm with friends and family about ways to honor their memory. Think about what they would have liked to have seen, or charities they would have wanted you to sponsor. Start a scholarship. Give to an existing charity in their name. Build a bench, plant a tree or garden, play a game, go on a trip, "do" something that gives space to your grief and enables you to express it, both individually and collectively, and carries on their legacy into the future. It's not a magic cure, and the "work of mourning" is hard, but it also helps us on our journey.

What does it mean to "celebrate" the life of the person who has just died? Talk of "celebration" in the aftermath of loss sounds odd and paradoxical. Celebration should not mean that we bypass grief or ignore the reality of the loss. Too often people want to skip grief and focus on celebration apart from grief. Instead, celebration means that we honor his or her memory in our grief. Through these tangible acts of remembrance we honor the person they were, with their unique gifts and abilities, and the way he or she enriched our lives. Celebration does not negate sadness: we still obviously miss them and mourn their loss, but it recognizes what their relationship meant to us and it can inspire us to live out our lives with purpose and meaning even if that relationship was conflicted and difficult. These types of activities and efforts help us to integrate our loss into our lives, to adjust to life without them, and it helps us keep their legacy alive long after they're gone.

EIGHT

PLAYING THROUGH THE PAIN

In sports, playing through the pain comes with the territory. You play through lingering injuries, aches, cuts, bruises, and sometimes much worse. The pages of sports lore are full of stirring stories of players who take a big hit or suffer a serious injury and come back into the game to spur their team onto victory. On the biggest stage in hockey, the Stanley Cup playoffs, Toronto Maple Leaf player Bobby Baun broke his leg, came back to the ice, and scored the game-winning goal—skating on a broken leg! His willingness to play through the pain exemplifies the sports values of courage, perseverance, and endurance, inspiring future generations of hockey players, whose instinct after an injury is always to get back onto the bench as soon as safely possible, and sometimes sooner!

In grief, too, we have to play through the pain in the sense that we have to go through life wounded not with a broken bone, but with a broken heart. It calls for courage, perseverance and endurance, as well as faith, hope, and love. As we mentioned above, people make all sorts of insensitive and ill-conceived comments to the bereaved. "When are you going to get over it?"; "Why don't you just move on with your life?"; "Have you healed yet?" These questions reveal the widespread misconceptions about the grieving process. You don't "get *over*" loss, you "learn to live with it". You don't "move *on*," you "move *with*" it. You don't "heal," you "*mend*," and only ever in part. You learn to live with your grief, to function with it, to cope with it, but you're forever changed. You're forever wounded and the rehab is life-long, but it doesn't mean you can't enjoy life and contribute to the lives of others, like Baun did with his broken leg. Even broken hearts can heal and love and laugh again. In fact, brokenness seems to enhance our ability to empathize, show compassion, and appreciate the richness, beauty, and fragility of life. It's the soil out of which a rich harvest of emotional and spiritual strength sprouts.

Playing through the pain also means recognizing that some days will be more painful than others. Birthdays, anniversaries, holidays, and other special or notable occasions often compound feelings of loss, sometimes to an emotional breaking point. We should anticipate these difficult times and come up with a game plan beforehand. Wayne Gretzky was famous for having a "sixth sense" or "eyes in the back of his head" because of his uncanny and unique ability to pass the puck to where his teammates were *going* rather than where they *were*. He had the gift of anticipation, which enabled him to make great plays by foreseeing how the situation would unfold. Similarly, we should plan out how we want to spend our time on days when we can expect heightened emotions, both for us and for others also facing similar challenges. What will you need on that day? Do you want to do some activity to mark the occasion or do you want to give yourself permission to take a break from the intensity of your grief and sadness that day? Do you want to be alone or do you want to be around others, and whom? What will your bereaved friends need? You should ask them if you can be helpful in any way on difficult days. Perhaps they need a listening ear. Perhaps they just need your presence. Perhaps they just want to go out and have fun. Be there for them.

We hope that these pages have given you some insights into loss and the life-long process of grieving. We encourage you to talk about your grief, to tell your story, to think about ways to express it concretely, and to lean on each other for support when the going gets tough. Your grief is yours alone, but you're not alone in grief. Never forget that.

NINE

OVERTIME

"There are more things in heaven and earth, Horatio,
Than are dreamt of in your philosophy"

— *Hamlet* 1.5.174–175

Games, like our lives, have a finite duration. They have beginnings and ends. Although we might wish they would last forever, eventually the buzzer sounds and the game's over. What happens after the cheering fades, the lights go out, and the doors close? The game might end, but the sport lives on. Sports with long and proud histories remind of us of their survival beyond the particular game and beyond the particular athletes of every generation. Sports sometimes help us reflect on the mystery of life, particularly life after death. Perhaps the most famous example of this is the beloved movie *Field of Dreams*.

In *Field of Dreams*, Ray Kinsella builds a baseball field in his cornfield at the behest of a mysterious voice despite the financial ruin it causes him. His behavior puzzles his pragmatic family and friends, but, as the movie unfolds, it's clear the field contains special power: it brings baseball players from the past into the present, and those with the right spiritual perception, those who have regained the lost innocence of childhood, are able to watch their past heroes. It's an idyllic film about redemption, reconciliation, and pursing your dreams, all within the broader frame of the love of baseball. It raises the questions that we'll reflect on in our final moments together: spirituality and the afterlife.

Many people are not comfortable talking about religion or spirituality. In fact, some are quite hostile to that sort of conversation, particularly when they're grieving. That's all right: we're not trying to force the conversation if you're not interested. You may simply not want to walk down that path at this time in your grief journey. Others are interested in spirituality, but don't really know what they believe. That's all right too: here we're talking more about grief and less about doctrine or even religion *per se*. Finally, some have strong beliefs but don't know how to reconcile them with their experience of loss. Here we'll give some initial thoughts on the relationship between grief and spirituality. It calls for a longer conversation, but we'll save that for another book.

The grief experience encompasses the whole person: body, mind, heart, and spirit or soul. We've spent most of our time talking about how to process grief practically, intellectually, and emotionally, but what about the soul? Grief confronts us with ultimate questions about the existence of God, the nature and meaning of life, and life after death. It provides an occasion (albeit unwelcome) to reconnect with our spiritual lives in order to find resources for coping with grief. Many people, for instance, find comfort in the belief that their loved one continues to exist in an afterlife, often called heaven. Also, many people talk about feeling God's comforting presence during times of grief. And yet, not everyone has religious beliefs. Here we want to talk about the connection between loss and spirituality at a general level as a primer for a later, fuller discussion.

Even if you have a strong faith or belief system, the reality of life after death does not take away the pain of the physical separation of our loved ones. No, their loss still hurts us now and it's no consolation in the moment to say we'll see them in heaven. We miss them now. We want to hold them and touch them and talk to them now, and so we grieve their absence in our lives. And yet, the belief that we'll reunite with them in heaven is a source of great joy and comfort amid our grief. So we have to balance the hope of heaven with the weight of grief, never using heaven to diminish the reality of grief and yet looking to heaven as a place where every tear will vanish (Revelation 21:4).

What will heaven be like? What will we look like? What will our loved ones look like? What will we do? We really don't know all the answers to these questions, but we're intrigued by them. The popularity of books such as *Heaven is For Real*, where a boy recounts his experience of heaven, reflects our interest in the fate of our souls after death. Heaven, in Christianity, is a place of healing, celebration, community, forgiveness, and unspeakable joy. The Bible says we cannot even think or imagine it because it's utterly beyond our comprehension (1 Corinthians 2:9). We are, however, given hints, echoes, and glimpses of eternity. The Bible uses lush imagery: vibrant colors, soaring music, and feasting. Think of the best party you've ever attended. Well, that doesn't even come close. That party might have included some of your best friends and lasted into the early morning hours, but this party will include all your favorite people in heaven and will never end. It's an eternal party. The celebration in heaven will make the best earthly parties you've ever had seem like afternoon tea at your Aunt Matilda's in comparison.

For some, however, talk of heaven rings hollow in moments of despair. They can't wait for the sweet by and by for comfort. They need to get through today, through this moment. Heaven's too remote and too abstract to bring any comfort. For some, they need a God who's with them right here and right now, not at some point in the distant future. That's why the suffering of Jesus is a source of spiritual strength and comfort for many Christians. God knows about suffering. God lost his Son, and Jesus, the Son of God, was tortured, suffered, and died. In a mysterious way, God suffers for us and with us, which means God is profoundly present with us in our suffering. The Bible says that God is close to the broken-hearted (Psalm 34:18) and comforts those who mourn (Matthew 5:4). Knowing that God suffers and that God is present with us in our anguish and suffering brings comfort to many. The famous *Footprints* picture artistically conveys God's presence with us in sorrow. Sometimes God walks beside us on our journey through grief, and sometimes He carries us when we're too weak to continue in our own strength.

You might not be very religious or religious at all. You might not be interested in spirituality. That's okay: we're not trying to push anything on you here. We do want to say, however, that grief encompasses the whole person, including the life of the soul. If you believe that you and your loved one are something more than blind matter in motion that simply perishes at death, then you'll have to process your loss at a spiritual level as well. It becomes an opportunity to access the resources of your religious tradition and to think through the broader questions about spirituality and life after death. We have found in our Christian faith a deep reservoir of truth to help us cope with our losses. We hope it's a good starting point for your reflection on these questions.

TEN

BREAKAWAY

I t's the most thrilling moment in sports. You break away from the defense and face the goalie one-on-one, mano-a-mano, a fight to the finish. It's a duel between you and their last line of defense. You fly in at full speed and make your move. A hush comes over the crowd before it explodes with applause or groans. It's all or nothing for both teams. A goal or save ensues in the flurry that follows, and either result sends the crowd to their feet in jubilation or despair. Breakaways are pivotal moments when the fate of the game rests in your hands, and that's a rush for any athlete. It's a make or break moment.

Here at the end of the book we want to leave you with a final encouragement. Loss doesn't have to mean the end of your life and the prospect of happiness in the future. How very sad when someone dies and the person left behind dies inside too. It's not what the departed person would want, and yet that scenario's all-too common. As your new life slowly unfolds, you can discover a world where hope, joy, and love blossom, if you open yourself to them. It takes a lot of hard work, the lifelong work of mourning, but it will help you enter into this new world. Alan Wolfelt says we have to mourn well to live well, so break away from the old misconceptions about sucking it up, stuffing it in, and going it alone and find a new way of life where you lean on your family, friends, counselors, support groups, and others, to find ways to express your grief and begin the life-long process of healing. You didn't choose your circumstance, but you do choose how you'll respond to it, and who you'll become in the process.

The game's on the line. It's up to you.

EULOGY FOR SUSIE

BY: MARK S. M. SCOTT

Norquay Lodge, Canmore, Alberta, February 26, 2008
Willow Creek Baptist Church, Midhurst, Ontario, March 01, 2008

Hear the words of the Apostle Paul in Romans 8:38–39: "For I am convinced that neither death nor life, neither angels nor demons, neither the present nor the future, nor any powers, neither height nor depth, nor anything else in all creation, will be able to separate us from the love of God that is in Christ Jesus our Lord." We gather together today to honour the memory of Susanna Helen Lantz. From far and wide we have come to celebrate her life and mourn her untimely death.

Susie's life is a love story. It is a love story inspired by and centered on her mom: Ruth Ann Lantz. In order to paint a complete picture of Susie, you would have to begin and end with her mom. Ruth was a saintly woman. Famous for her big hugs and big smile, Ruth was a light that warmed the hearts of those around her, bringing joy to all she met. She imparted these qualities to Susie. When Ruth died at Susie's side 11 years ago, part of Susie went with her and only part of her remained here with us. But even with a broken heart Susie had so much love to give to us, and the wellspring of that love was her mom. Now at long last they are reunited forever, locked in joyous embrace, waiting for us to join the eternal circle of love and laughter in heaven through God's grace.

And as in any great love story, there's a cast of supporting characters that play a vital role. Her three sisters are absolutely central to her story. Tom rightly remarked the other day that it doesn't take too long to figure out that the Lantz girls are special people. Susie loved and was loved by her sisters. She had a unique relationship with each of them. Deb was her kindred spirit, her partner in adventure, and her source for wisdom and advice. Esther was her faithful friend, a listening ear, and a constant source of encouragement. Bethany was her first best friend, her accomplice in fun and "girl stuff," and her close confidant. Jim, her father, was her steadfast supporter and encourager, a faithful prayer warrior, and her greatest fan. And all of us here, friends and family, fill out the cast of her beautiful story. Your presence here is a testimony to her legacy of love, a legacy bequeathed by her mom, cultivated by her family, and dispersed generously to all of us. We will honour her memory if we continue her legacy of love in our lives.

Her love story doesn't end here. She has left imprints on our hearts that will stay with us forever. We come here tonight with our own life story, but tonight our stories converge. Tonight we are one. Tonight we are "Team Susie." Her love for us and our love for her is stronger than the driven snow, stronger than any avalanche, stronger than death itself.

Susanna Helen Lantz: our dearly beloved Susie. A shooting star, she graced our skies with her light for a moment, filling us with joy and wonder, leaving us longing for more.

"Come back to us if you can. We'll look for you in the freshly fallen snow, when we get on our bicycles, when we plant a tree. When we're climbing we'll feel your warmth on the sun bathed rock and hear your encouraging voice. When we're competing we'll think of your drive and determination. We'll wrap ourselves up in your scarves and reread the stories and kind words you've written us and we'll love you all over again. Come back to us Susie"

—Deborah Lantz

MY GAME PLAN FOR GRIEF: A CHECKLIST

RESOURCES:

1. Teammates: friends and family to walk beside me on my grief journey.

    a.

    b.

    c.

    d.

2. Strategies: ways to take care of myself as I cope with my grief.

    a.

    b.

    c.

    d.

3. Professional help that might guide me through my grief journey.

   a. Professional counseling.

   b. Grief counseling (individual).

   c. Grief counseling (support groups).

   d. Pastoral counseling.

ACTION PLAN:

COMMUNICATION:

1. Ways to express my grief/tell my story (e.g., journaling, poetry, art, conversation).

   a.

   b.

   c.

   d.

2. People to reach out to and to listen to their story.

   a.

   b.

   c.

   d.

3. People to stay in close contact with, keep lines of communication open.

    a.

    b.

    c.

    d.

PRESENCE:

1. Who might I allow to be present for me in my grief journey?

    a.

    b.

    c.

    d.

2. Who might I be present for in their grief journey?

    a.

    b.

    c.

    d.

1. Think of meaningful ways to express my love/grief.

   a.

   b.

   c.

   d.

2. Keep them present in my life through actions/tributes/memorials.

   a.

   b.

   c.

   d.

3. How am I different now that they are gone physically?

   a.

   b.

   c.

   d.

4. List the ways they enriched my life. How did they change me?

   a.

   b.

   c.

   d.

WORKS ON DEATH, LOSS, AND GRIEF

Attig, T., *The Heart of Grief; How We Grieve*

Beder, J. *Voices of Bereavement: A Casebook for Grief Counselors*

Burpo, T. and L. Vincent, *Heaven is for Real*

Buckle, Jennifer L. and Stephen J. Fleming, *Parenting After the Death of a Child*

Doka, Kenneth J., *Disenfranchised Grief: Hidden Sorrow*

Haugk, Kenneth C., *Journeying Through Grief*

Jeffreys, J. S., *Helping Grieving People*

Kushner, H., *When Bad Things Happen to Good People*

Lewis, C. S., *A Grief Observed; The Problem of Pain*

Manning, Doug, *The Gift of Significance*

Maxwell, John C., *Leadership Gold*

McMahon, R.and Persson, K., *Good Mourning: A Resource for Healing* Millar, William, *When Going to Pieces Keeps you Together*

Moffat, M. J., ed., *In the Midst of Winter*

Morse, M., *Closer to the Light*

Perschey, M., *Helping Teens Work through Grief*

Putter, A. M., ed., *The Memorial Rituals Book for Healing and Hope*

Romain, T., *What on Earth Do You Do When Someone Dies?*

Walsh, M. and McGoldrich, eds., *Living Beyond Loss*

Wolterstorff, Nicholas, *Lament for a Son*

Wolfelt, Alan, *Understanding Your Grief*

Worden, J. M., *Grief Counseling and Grief Therapy*

NOTES

NOTES

NOTES

NOTES

NOTES

NOTES

NOTES

NOTES

NOTES

NOTES

CPSIA information can be obtained at www.ICGtesting.com
Printed in the USA
LVOW12s1036311214

420967LV00005B/232/P